In My Comfort Zone

A collection of poetry and writings
By
Mary A. Dailey

ISBN 978-0-615-28348-7

On The Cover: "The Dailey Family Pond"

Beached

I reclined on a large beach towel in amazement, admiring the prettiest pale blue sky I've ever seen. Everything seemed calm and peaceful, along the shore of Pensacola Beach. I took a deep breath and the warm salty air not only cleared my sinuses but cleared my head of the hustle and bustle I'd left behind. As the beaming sun rays absorbed into my well-oiled skin, the subtle breeze provided a comfortable medium. I closed my eyes, dug my heels in the sugar white sand and wiggled my toes in search of cool moistness below the surface. The soothing sounds of the ocean and passing seagulls carried me out to sea and into my comfort zone.

CONTENTS
Acknowledgements
Introduction

Chapter One
Life

Chapter Two
Folklore

Chapter Three
Love

Chapter Four
Spirituality

To
My loving parents, Lizzie Mae and Jethro Dailey Sr.,
The memory of my beloved grandparents, Mary and Richard Jackson
My treasures, Eric and Thaddeus
My extended treasures, Nicholas, Frederick, Steven and Travis
Love and fond memories of Anthony and Elizabeth
A special thanks to Mr. Adrian A. Abrams, book cover design
My family, friends and co-workers,
All whose laughter and tears brought to my remembrance,
Hope and encouragement

Introduction

I believe that my never ending passion for life somehow evolved from my childhood and that there is a corner of my mind reserved strictly for such lasting fond memories. So let me set the tone for what you're about to read. I make no excuse for my repetitious references to nature in this book. When looking back over my life, the first thing that comes to mind is the great outdoors, endless summer days…hot and humid. It wasn't unusual to spend the entire day outdoors, playing games like hopscotch, no walking-no talking-no showing your teeth, bobby jacks on the back porch, tag and hide and seek till dark. Momma would call us in for supper and we'd slip right back out. I believe my momma was one of the best cooks in town. I'd put her buttermilk cornbread, navy beans, pinto beans, slaw, turnip, collards and mustard greens, pork chops, pot roast, fried chicken, banana pudding, sweet potato pies and cakes up against anyone's-including my grandma Mary's, who was a darn good cook. There was dessert with almost every evening meal. Rest assured, if she didn't cook dessert, Daddy had some cherry vanilla ice-cream stashed away in the freezer. At Christmas time, there was baked ham, turkey and dressing. Traditional yes, and so much more. Topped off with desserts, to make any child smile, six or seven cakes-including her rum soaked fruit cake and assorted pies. Each a sought after delicacy. Sometimes, gracing our dining room table would even be roasted wild game of some sort, sporting a sweet potato in its mouth. Not to mention, the deer tender loin, and mouth-dripping fried rabbit smothered in onion gravy with biscuits.

Some days, while walking the dusty red clay roads of South Alabama, after playing with cousins and the neighbor's children, rain would meet us like a giant curtain. We'd hurriedly get home and gather the clothes from the clothes line so Momma wouldn't know we didn't get them in when she told us to. After a long hot summer's day of fun, bath time was just as much fun, improvised from Momma's laundry detergent or dish washing liquid to create the ultimate bubble bath. Of course, Momma wasn't looking. It's a wonder I have any skin at all now that I think back at how harsh those detergents were. Can you imagine a bubble bath with Tide? Most of my Saturdays; however were spent preparing for church. There was Mom's Saturday morning pressing and curling hair; and with her being the community beautician and seamstress, we wore the prettiest of dresses…rows of lace, ruffles, hair bows and bobby socks. I never considered myself poor and to look at any of her eleven children, you wouldn't either. There was Sunday school and church at the Mt. Gilead Missionary Baptist Church. I thank God for parents who instilled in me biblical based ethics. Sometimes it seemed as if we were in church all day. Sometimes we were in church all day; but never hungry before Sunday dinner was served, thanks to Momma. I can recall as if it were yesterday, Sunday mornings, as the delectable aroma of her fried chicken, homemade macaroni and cheese, biscuits and gravy circulated subtly after having escaped the stove top. Sometimes it traveled aggressively nonstop throughout the house and eventually seeped underneath my bedroom door. Talk about recycling…my Momma recycled before there was ever a need to recycle. We used leftover biscuits to shine our patent leather church shoes.

I grew up in the Deep South, Atmore, Alabama. The population was about thirty thousand. Whenever someone asked where it's located, the best way to tell them is to say that it's about 54 miles northeast of Mobile, Alabama. I had my share of working the fields. Picking cucumbers, potatoes, chopping soybeans, and in the fall of the year, stripping sugar cane at Granddaddy Richard's syrup mill. I often prayed for rain. Thank God I never had the pleasure of picking cotton, as did my older sisters. Hard work didn't kill me. It taught me to appreciate my present day office job, in a climate controlled building [Thank You Lord]. It also taught me to appreciate the value of a dollar and a very, very comfortable place to live. There was lots of creek bank fishing just off the dusty red clay roads of the community of Freemanville, deep sea fishing in Pensacola, Florida's Gulf of Mexico, lots of dew covered blades of green grass and mud between my toes, blistering hot sand underneath my bare feet and let's not forget the ultimate ocean side church picnic with barbeque and Momma's best potato salad. Sometimes when I've been most troubled by life's circumstances, I've often closed my eyes in an effort to mentally journey back to those days. It is my sincere hope that this book of poetry and writings will not only inspire you but encourage you. So, journey with me through my childhood days and life thereafter.

Chapter One

Life

It would probably take me a lifetime to expound upon life's experiences. So I will only share what I consider "the most important things in life". How we live shapes the very essence of our lives. The bible states, "Man who is born of a woman is of few days and full of trouble. He comes forth like a flower and fades away". From the very moment we enter this world, we are dying. The aging process doesn't cease until life cease to exist. And even then, the mortal body will continue to decompose. Time waits for no one. We are born, we live and then we die. We should be grateful for every thing we experience in life, whether good or bad. The bad gives us a greater appreciation for the good. I cherish those days of my childhood most because life was so simple, sweet and innocent. If only we adults were more like children. We would harbor less bitterness, be more forgiving and wouldn't have half the health problems.

Every one of us, at some point in our lives, will go through a storm of some sort, strong enough to rock the foundation of our being; it is an inevitable part of life. How we handle the difficult times directly translates to our survival rate and quality of life afterwards. There have been some situations in my adult life that I would like very much to forget. But there are also some memories of my childhood I wouldn't trade for anything in this world.

What I've learned…
I've learned that it's okay to cry. God has given us the avenue of tears…but don't stay there too long. Pray and move on. Healing must take place if you really expect to survive. To find true happiness…learn how to live and not just exist. Don't inhale just

to exhale because respiration is necessary in life…BREATHE. Trust God with everything.

Ecclesiastes 3:1 states, "To every thing there is a season, a time for every purpose under heaven." I sincerely believe that it is my season, to heal, to grow, to prosper and to love. Come go with me, and let this be our season to live as we look back on life's experiences.

In My Comfort Zone

An unforeseen storm raged
Leaving lives torn apart
Giving into a broken spirit
Only hastened a hurting heart

In search of shelter from the storm
Feeling abandoned and all alone
I resorted to the one thing I knew
The Sweetest Name I'd ever known

Captivated by time and nature
Entertaining a world of my own
With pen in hand my journey began
As I entered my comfort zone

I returned enchantingly to my childhood
Suddenly it was if my soul was set free
Not a care in the world for all was well
With my mind, my spirit and me

Hours soon turned into days
Weeks to months, then years
While journaling seemingly sooth my heart
The Master was drying my tears
Time stood still just long enough
For me to appreciate this time alone
So listen to the rhythm of peace and solitude
In the journals of my comfort zone

Happiness Is

Happiness is...
Being grateful for my ability to watch the beautiful sunrise every
morning
Listening to the rain and allowing the rhythmic sound to comfort
you
Watching the snow fall...appreciating its calming effect and
staying warm
Knowing with each day there will be challenges; but there is
nothing too hard for God

Happiness is...
Having peace and having real joy, finding joy in simple things,
Regardless of the circumstance, there is something on the inside no
one can take away

Happiness Is...
The ability to love and holding no malice in your heart
Loving whether it be a maternal instinct, Eros and/or Agape
And although you love, you have the courage to let go

Happiness Is...
Having a forgiving heart
Having a passion for life
Having a desire to really live and not just to exist

I Dream In Color

I use to fall asleep at night
In tearful nightmares of black and white
Now I wake up with a great big smile
After beckoning dreams to last awhile
I now dream in color

Sometimes awakened by laughter
Coveting a life happily ever after
Overjoyed-oh for the life of me
I would love to display for all to see
Those dreams in color

Thank you Lord for giving me hope
When I'd ultimately reached the end of my rope
Oh to feel youthful, young and so free
I can't help but praise him for such liberty
When I dream in color

I'm There

I closed my eyes and my imagination soared
Through the meadows of my childhood days
I stood barefoot in a field of wildflowers
Near the pastures where the oxen grazed

Sunflowers, daffodils and buttercups danced
An old tire-swing roped to a big oak tree
Pretty blue skies dawned before my eyes
While listening to a songbird's melody

In the distant skies the crop duster flew
The soybean fields were vibrant and green
Honeysuckles draped all along the fencerow
The most beautiful thing I'd ever seen

Beneath the thickets, a robin scurried
The blackberries grew wild and care free
The morning dew revived the large cornfields
As the smell of His fresh air intoxicated me

Lifting my face to the sun, I thanked God
An awesomeness that only He could unfold
What a bountiful richness I've found in nature
And just imagine…His likeness I long to behold

Though miles and years separate us now
I can find it all again from almost anywhere
Whenever I need a quick get away from it all
I simply close my eyes and imagine I'm there

Heart Leaps

My heart leaps with anticipation
Of days to come, new life and such
Hard to limit the imagination
When a Devine hand has truly touched
My destiny…
Oops, there goes another one!
I'm still growing in leaps and bounds
Hard to sit still and keep my feet on the ground
When my heart leaps

A Summer's Day

The thick humidity moistens my skin
After a cadence of steady rain is gone
I could fall asleep in Grandpa's old hammock
If the gnats and mosquitoes would leave me alone

The smell of fresh air after a summer's rain
Soft pedals gently blowing in a subtle breeze
Watch a modest butterfly masterfully float about
Shhhhh! Listen to the flight of a real bumblebee

The hummingbirds frozen in mid-air sipping;
The mid-day heat rapidly dries up the residue
How could anyone fail to tell God Thanks?
When He places such awesomeness in view

Swoosh! The freshwater fish grab food from the surface
When I look up, only the ripple flows free
A large frog watches over the pond on a lily pad
Resembling the captain of a small vessel-headed out to sea.

Slowly but surely another day comes to an end
Crickets come out for their nightly revival
With lightening bugs carrying the torch
Signaling the night's arrival.

As the sun slowly sets over the distant sky
I say goodnight to another summer's day

What I Like

I like ice cream and cookies at bedtime
A Swiss mocha or crème latte' in my cup
I just shake the crumbs from my bed sheets
And politely dust my pillow when I get up

The sound of rainfall on a tin roof
While being somewhere safe and warm
My favorite pajamas and a good book
Good company amidst a quiet storm

Holding hands with a close friend
No words needed to communicate
A heartfelt smile, thumbs up
A visit that's always worth the wait

Fishing trips to a slow creek bank
A take-along lunch or a snack
Souse meat, cheese, bologna and crackers
All in a greasy brown paper sack

The many sounds of the great outdoors
Lightening bugs, crickets and frogs
After late summer and fall have ended;
Sparks of light from a campfire's log

Laughter, till I get cramps in my stomach
A good cry or rain, every now and then
Either will do to wash debris away
So hurting hearts can finally mend
This is what I like.

Life's Experiences

I've watched the sunset in the distant skies
I've cooled my heals in a running stream
I've listened to God speak through nature
And I've found pleasure in simple things

I met my first love while in the park
I've stolen a kiss under the starry skies
Been punished for staying out too late
And for telling some really tall lies

I've shown love and been in love
With someone I thought was true
I've been hurt by someone I've trusted
And been betrayed by more than a few

I've flown across the Pacific Ocean
I've walked on foreign soil
I've sailed across the Gulf of Mexico
Watching the waves of a vast sea toil

I've brought a life into this world
I've cried as I've watched one expire
I've said good-bye to a dying loved one
And I've found joy watching one retire

I've listened to secret details of a first love
And proud of all those secrets I've kept
I've held a newborn babe in my arms
And prayed for one while they slept

Life's experiences have taught me well
Seen more than I thought I'd ever see
To have lived, loved and grown in grace
I'm just thankful for what God's done for me

So Turn the Page

Tender moments shared, treasured from the start
Made sense in your head but challenged your heart
Destined to move forward, you refused to give in
God has written your story and this isn't how it ends
So close the chapter, turn the page, brave soul move on
Heartache is but temporary, it comes only to make you strong

Bound by kindred spirits more often than you know
Subdue untimely passion and watch a friendship grow
Just down the road a bit and over a fence or two
Lies green pastures and quiet streams calling out to someone like you

So close the chapter, turn the page,
you'll never have it-if you don't move on
Eventually it will come to you
and praying it won't be long

If doubts dim the progress made while awaiting a heart to mend
Measure the distance from where you are and compare it to where
you've been

A shield from the wind and rain, a constant friend indeed
The table is set before you now and that's all you'll ever need
So close this chapter, you've got to turn the page
If you're expecting to move on
You don't have to read between the lines
To find you're not alone

Just turn the page

Chapter Two

Folklore

Okay, I know. You're probably wondering, "Where is she going with this?"

We all have them.

It's the folks in the neighborhood and our families that we won't ever forget.

Regardless of where you grew up, there was a bootlegger, a town gossiper, the preacher and/or teacher who inspired you, and for some reason, we won't ever forget,…the town drunk.

If it wasn't the town drunk, there were others (more than likely) that we are too embarrassed to talk about because they're related to us.

Let's face it, we weren't always as "polished" as we are today. So my advice to you is to embrace your past. In some way or another, these people, places and things helped shape our lives.

If you haven't figured it out yet, just turn the page.

Aunt Mabel's Place

Down in the deep country
You could hear the jukebox real loud
Aunt Mabel ran a juke joint
In my little tiny hometown
Mr. Fisher was sho gettin loaded
Junior Lee was dancing a jig
Miss Bee was pretending she didn't see a thing
And Cousin Tootsie had lost her wig
At Aunt Mabel's Place
They called my Aunt Mabel "Wild Bill"
She wore cowboy boots with her skirt
Black lace see-thru blouses and wigs
And oh how all the men would flirt
I could stand on my front porch and dance awhile
To Clarence Carter's "Let's Slip Away"
And that's exactly what Aunt Mabel did
With the money at the end of the day
At Aunt Mabel's Place
Every night was a party night
When the jukebox was all wound up
You really could "cut that rug" all night
While Aunt Mabel was filling your cup
You could hear the music from miles around
The jukebox was just a thumpin
The people would laugh and talk for hours
Freemanville was shone-nuff jumpin'
You could always have a good time
At Aunt Mabel's place
Aunt Mabel was the life of the party
Every now and then even she'd take a nip
Edna's eyes rolled back in her head
Gold-tooth Sadie was on the dance floor letting it rip
Round twelve or so they were all give out
Their parties never last that long
Mr. Johnson made sure nothing was left
So he drank till all the liquor was gone
At Aunt Mabel's place
It's been years since, Aunt Mabel's passed
Now stands a beauty salon
But I'm sure her spirit still roams about
When the customers have all gone home
After all…this was…Aunt Mabel's place

Silly Sallie

Silly Sallie had a man
He beat her every night
You could hear her scream for miles
She never put up a fight
Silly Sallie had a man
But he would no longer be the only one
She put on her good clothes and went out on the town
She decided to have some fun
When her drunken man found out
He beat her till she could hardly see
He broke her arm in three places
And how her nose did bleed
Silly Sallie, a battered woman
She'd finally had enough
She watched him play poker with his buddies
He dranked and dipped his snuff
Silly Sallie had a plan
When he got drunk and fell asleep
She tied him to the bedpost
And listened as the kettle steeped
He woke up to scalding water
She dashed him real good you see
She said, "This isn't just for the other women-oh no
This is also for the woman in me!"
Silly Sallie went to jail
The neighbors cheered her all the way
She did some time for being evil
But she got her revenge that day
So if you marry a Silly Sallie
Don't ever try to beat her
The tables just may turn someday
So be careful how you treat her

14

The Clothes Line Dance

When momma wasn't looking, I shook her clothes line
I grabbed a bucket, turn it up and made the clothes dance
They were forced to move to my own smooth grove
I had to do it before my momma took a second glance

The blue dress curtsied while the knit pants bowed
The long johns were swaying to the overhaul's bop
The bloomers and boxers had absolutely no shame
While the red dress did the shimmy and wouldn't stop

The stockings swiveled and swirled all about
The mismatched socks seemed to all be confused
The under slips moved as though light as a feather
While the clothes on the other end got the news

Look at Mr. Blue Shirt, stuck one sleeve in his pocket
And then Miss Miniskirt did her own little shout
Moving and grooving while staying in the line
But then the khaki's on the end turned it all out

"Shake it baby-shake it" that's what I said to the line
The Blue jeans danced like they were husband and wife
The nightcaps were giddy while the nightgowns huddled
And the poor clothespins were hanging on for dear life

Ode to Momma's clothesline, we had a good ole time
They were moving like zombies in a trance
Thank God Momma never found out the clothes were all out
In the backyard doing the clothes line dance

The Night Junior Lee Turned Into a Cat

Out on the town with his homey
Cousin Johnny was so high,
Walking the long way home
He turned to his left, then to his right
And he freaked cause Junior Lee was gone

Now ole tales speak of spooks and goblins
But we wouldn't know 'bout all that
All we have is Cousin Johnny's account
Of the night Junior Lee turned into a cat

He ran to cousin Mildred's house
And said, "Come and see for yourself!"
They laughed cause Cousin Johnny was drunk
But for some reason was the only one left

Dazed and confused about the occurrence
He scratched his head and tossed his hat
He peed in his pants as he hauled ass
Cause Junior Lee had turned into a cat

Cousin Johnny's gone on to the great beyond
But who could even fathom a tale like that
To his grave the only eye-witness account
Of the night Junior Lee turned into a cat

Childhood Games

Here We Go 'round the Mulberry Bush
Can you play one called Hide and Seek?
Childhood games, what's my name?
No walking, no talking, no showing your teeth!

Jumping Jacks, Hopscotch, Double Dutch
Bouncing to the Baby Bop!
Which game would you like to play today?
Red light, Green light, Stop!

Lil Sally Walker sitting in a saucer
Ride Sally Ride let's see
Andy and Allyson sitting in a tree
K-I-S-S-I-N-G!

Mary Mack Dressed in Black
Silver buttons all down her back
It didn't cost a dime and they were such a hit
I got you now boy "Tag, You're It!"

Take me back to my childhood days
Things were much easier back then
Life was simple, life was innocent
Those childhood games we could win

Grandma's Chickens

My Grandma raised a whole lot of chickens
They dapped around the backyard all day
They gathered on the back porch for their breakfast
Resembling a church contest giveaway
Grandma never had to set the alarm clock
Five o'clock and she never overslept
Now I know why the hens lost their lives
But all the rooster's lives were kept
We took turns gathering eggs for breakfast
Sometimes the hens would angrily attack
Whenever I got caught out in the henhouse
I'd be running with a chicken pecking my back
Sometimes the roosters would get into a big fight
While the grandchildren would gather around
We named them "Big Red" and "Cockatoo"
It must have been the greatest event in town
I never knew why the roosters were fighting
I guess it had to do with who'd give the wake up call
Well, anyway while they'd be going at it
My cousins and I placed bets on who would fall
One day Big Red raised his dusty feathers
Cockatoo was scratching up the ground
The hens resembled little women murmuring
Whispering about the big fight going down
Big Red got the best of ole Cockatoo
Before Grandma's broomstick could break up the fight
If she hadn't interrupted them when she did
We would have plucked and ate chicken that night
I won't ever forget Grandma's Chickens
Funny how similar our lives are today
If we don't stop the fighting one another
We'll end up on the devil's plate

Granddaddy Richard

Granddaddy Richard, the slowest man in town, a good mechanic he'd profess to be
He'd fixed your car for only a few bucks and he'd tell you that's all it would be
He'd take a nap between each job; He'd make you want to lose your mind
He might not remember where he put the keys, be patient and give him some time

Granddaddy Richard, the slowest man in town, he was quite outspoken you see
He told tall tales about goblins and ghost, he scared the pure heck out of me
Because we were children, he told those tales, we believed everything he said
If he forgot how the story ended that day, he would just laugh and scratch his head

Granddaddy Richard, the slowest man in town, played checkers at the corner grocery
store
What I wouldn't give to see him again, to hear his grubby little voice once more
He made a lot of friends over the years; he was everybody's mechanic you see
If you had the time, he would do just fine but he'd tell you that it sure wasn't free

Granddaddy Richard, the slowest man in town, got old one day and had to be put in a
home
He flirted with the nurses and had a good time, even though he complained about being
alone
He was very frank and he spoke his mind, didn't mind being somewhat overt
But we knew he loved us he was just plain honest, no matter who's feelings he hurt

Granddaddy Richard, the slowest man in town, you had to have patience to conversate
When he spoke it was slow but plain, he was a good man, make no mistake
One day the Lord called him home; and I know for sure he's real happy up there
He's probably fixing on the angels' wings, and he'll put them back if he can remember
where

Granddaddy Richard, the slowest man in town, it took him awhile to do anything-you
see
I can laugh right now about how slow he was, he is still an inevitable part of me
Granddaddy, you were so, so, so slow, I inherited a whole lot of things from you
I can't complain about how long it took you to do anything, you see I'm real slow too

Chapter Three

Love

There have been more songs written about it than any other subject. I believe the Apostle Paul said it best in I Corinthians 13, one of the most beautiful and powerful odes to love ever written. "Bears all things, believes all things, hopes all things, endures all things."

Remember the first time I fell in love, I was twelve years old. At the time, it was as real as real could get. When I look back now, it was really more of an infatuation than anything. I laugh now when I think about how silly I was. My little knobby knees shook at the very thought of him. We spent countless hours writing silly love letters, poems, trading sentiments and making "say nothing" phone calls. I can recall asking permission to go the community park with my cousin Annie Ruth so I could meet him. Momma gave me specific instructions to be back before dark and guess what? I missed my curfew and I was scared to death. Momma met me in the middle of the road, walking towards home at dusk dark. Now some may indeed fear the wrath of God, but that night…I feared the "wrath of momma". I was in big trouble.

The power of love is amazing. When you give love, it warms your heart. When you're in love, it seems as if the sun is always shining. But when you long for love, amidst a life of loneliness, it seems as if the rain will never end. In the event of rain, be not discouraged dear one. Let prayer be your initial response, and seeking solace in our heavenly father, be your aim. He will give you exactly what is needed, when it is needed. Secondly, rather than being consumed by self-pity or depending on others to pull you out of the misery; take out pen and paper and write till your heart is content. I have found it to be good therapy.

What I've learned…
Love was never meant to be dirty or ugly. We humans created that
monster. Various forms of love can be beautiful when expressed
in its proper place and time.

Keep It Right There

"Keep it right there"
So often said to me
I've frozen in my footsteps
While daring my heart to see

Keep it right there
Can't take another step
Never kiss and tell anyone
So all my secrets were kept

Keep it right there
Tho wishing you were mine
Fond memories I will hold close
Done without crossing a line

Keep it right there
Don't let right become wrong
Hold on to the closeness shared
Binding a friendship strong

Keep it right there
A love simple, sweet and pure
Passion can sometimes blind you
When the heart is not so sure

Keep it right there
No matter how long it takes
A real love will last forever
When more than eros wakes

Gardenia Blossoms

A flawless flaunted fragrance
In the locks of ages past
Cradled in a crystal dish
Just to see how long you'd last
Your aromas demands attention
Your passion exudes aloud
Deep South's grow twenty high
And Billie wore you proud
A password for potter's mitt
An adoring wedding décor
Masses stored on parade
Imitated to linger more
Sensuous yet sentimental
Dynamics of diary and pen
Pressed and stored amongst the pages
Remembrance of way back when
You're as graceful as ever
Salutations to morning's dew
Lilies hmm; who needs them?
When I can lay eyes on you
My sweet Gardenia blossom
I just close my eyes and inhale
your fragrance.

There Goes the Rain Again

There goes the rain again
I really don't know how to explain
Why the sound of it woos me so
Makes me want to do some crazy things
Reflections of light on my face this morning
Remembering the night before
How the rain had begun to fall
When I said good-bye to you at the door

There goes the rain again
Let's turn around and go back inside
I want you to hold me close again
My feelings I can no longer hide
I wanted to get soaked in the rain with you
I wanted to dance till the break of dawn
An instant attraction when we met
Listening to the rain's rhythmic song

There goes the rain again
As you gently kissed my lips
Your hand tenderly brushed my face
Then traced it with fingertips

There goes the rain again
It always stirs such passion in me
Making it difficult to say goodnight
Not wanting you to let go of me
And now, I really don't want to be alone again...
While listening to the rain

At Midnight

At midnight I was awaken, heart palpitations
Thoughts of you make no mistake
My eyes came open, no words spoken
So mellow that I just couldn't wait

Call out to me again my sweet love
Your tender lips I'm longing to kiss
Dark eyes that could find real hope in mine
And a smile I find hard to resist

Hands so warm and inviting
They gently brushed my face
Strong arms holding, the night unfolding
Longing for happiness time can't erase

Visions of you oh so vivid
Standing in a silhouette of night
It must have been fate; I just couldn't wait
To have you hold me so tight

Now reminiscent of those tender hours
And with those memories I won't ever part
No longer in despair, because you are there
And at midnight...you stole my heart

You Move Me

You move me
You take me to places and spaces where voids use to be
You give me blue skies, butterflies in open fields of liberty
With un-earthen treasures and full pleasures
Crème filled chocolate spaces havened in a trance
A heart singing like Beethoven's Fifth Symphony
Wild goose bumps in novels of sweet romance

You move me
Like no other, to unexplored territory
In your arms eternal flames ignite
Sweet herbs and spices are adorn
In my secret garden as hearts take flight

You really move me
Dispelling all myths and disbeliefs
Of love undefiled and such
Like a single white rose cradling morning dew
Unknown to human touch

Because you move me
A major find occurs that defies all laws of nature
Thought only to exist in ages past
Only time will prove its longevity
Only if it's real will it last

A Birthday Poem for You
(A poem written for a dear friend's birthday, January 2005)

In the dead of winter
The midwife answered a call
Off to your family's household
Black medicine bag and all
Momma was indeed in labor
Pain fifteen minutes apart
Boy or Girl, it really didn't matter
Whoever would have her heart
And finally, he appeared
A beautiful baby boy made way
Momma sighed in sweet relief
Over forty years ago this day
Examining hand and feet
She counted ten fingers, ten toes
Deep brown beautiful eyes
Subtle skin and tiny little nose
Responding to her voice,
Only one eye opened a while
Making sure she was still there
Then giving her an angel's smile
"Go to sleep little baby", she'd sang
As silent tears of joy gave way
She prayed as he slept in her arms
"Lord, bless my baby boy this day"
Tiny hands, what will you do in life
Tiny feet, how fast will you grow
Whatever you decide to do in life
Take God with you as you go
And to this day, she still smiles
Her baby boy is all grown up
and he's made her very proud
Happy Birthday!!!

Holding My Hand

When my life really started to fall apart
You took my hand and held it secure
You taught me the real meaning of friendship
You kept it real, passionate but pure

You held my hand in some pretty rough times
Only letting go long enough to wipe my tears
You even held my hand and watched me grow
Now seems like you've been holding it for years

Whenever I became vulnerable and foolish
You looked beyond those simple things to see
What beauty was blossoming on the inside
You've always brought out the best in me

Finding words that so often encouraged
Not even emotions got in the way
Now that it's time to let go of you
I still look for reasons to have you stay

Years from now, even if we're miles apart
I'd like to know you're still holding on
With spiritual ties that will always bind us
With an agape love always sound and strong

Just keep holding my hand

Chapter Four

Spirituality

I sincerely believe that ultimate transformation of a Christian's life is evident when one views the world through the eyes of faith. My gratitude is for parents who nurtured me in the fear and admonition of the Lord. This is expressed throughout this book of poetry and writings. For it was in those adolescent years that I was first introduced to the Creator of the Universe, the Lamb of God, and the Comforter. However, it wasn't until I left home that I came to realize who was really in control of my destiny. I came to realize who the giver of life is, my sustainer, my joy and real hope for all my tomorrows.

In adversities, He has proven to be a strong tower. At my weakest, He has proven to be an inevitable source of strength. When I called, He answered. I could have easily given up and lost hope but I thank God for His amazing grace and mercy. There are no words to describe how low I've been, nor words to do justice to heights He's lifted me. Proverbs 22:6 says, "Train up a child in the way he should go, And when he is old he will not depart from it." As an adult, I've been in situations where some folks would have absolutely lost their mind. I sincerely believe learning how to pray and trusting God at an early age saved me from this world but mostly, saved me from myself.

What I've learned...
You can talk about religion all day but unless you have a personal relationship with God, you will never ever experience real love. You will only resemble "sounding brass and tinkling symbols" (I Corinthians 13).

God Is Awesome

Every now and then, he comes in like a flood and moistens my dull dry
attitude
It leaves me refreshed and anew just like the grass in the morning dew
He allows his angels to keep charge over me everyday and every night
while I'm asleep
He blows his breath in my face and I awaken every morning stronger
than the day before
My keeper and my sustainer, who could ask for anything more?
Sometimes, when I'm in my storm, I feel so all alone
I keep saying he's moving too slow and I really want to give him a hand
He says, "Don't interfere in what I'm doing, don't you know Who I am?"

I lean to the left and to the right trying to see what's ahead
and he says to me, "be patient, trust me, I got this!"

We spend half our lives rushing into things
The other half we spend trying to figure out
how to get out of things we've gotten ourselves in
If we would only stop to pray, leave it there
then and only then would we win
Every now and then.

God is awesome.

By The Ocean

I decided to take a trip down south
I just needed some time away
My heart had fallen and by the ocean God was calling
And I heard Him call my name that day

I arrived at the beach all alone
Listening to the vast ocean's roar
It was just so appealing to hear God revealing
As He said "Come with me along the shore"

Deeply troubled with nowhere else to turn
All I needed to hear was one word
I looked at the sea that he made just for me
And as he spoke by the ocean I heard

He said, "I am God and you are my child
And all your cares to me you should bring
If you're going to pray then do it my way
You've got to learn to let go of some things"

I was needlessly carrying weights around
Often standing with my back against a wall
So many wasted years and some senseless tears
Not realizing all I had to do was just call

I stood barefoot in the sand as the tides rolled in
I closed my eyes as the currents drifted me
With the wind in my hair, inhaling the warm salty air
The waves carried all my troubles out to sea

One Step Closer

One step closer to my destination
A milestone from an irrelevant past
Unimportant is the length of the distance
Insignificant is the time it will last
A few more steps and it's over
Seems like it has lasted some years
Loosen my sandals; wipe my brow
God's holding a canteen of my tears
Just a few more steps-I do believe
And the promises of God are all mine
Not to make naught of his promises
By recollecting what was left behind
Manifold treasures restored unto me
Manifold blessings yet to be.
Trying hard not to burst with excitement
With every thing said
But not yet done
I am here
One step closer

To Move

To move from this place
I must really want to let go
Of a past that has robbed me
And unconsciously stunted my growth
To move from this place
There must be a definite need
To be free of a memory
Suppressing a desire to succeed
To move from this place
Means I cannot go back
To a time of disillusionment
Leaving me totally off track
To move from this place
Means I cannot hold on
To people, places and things
Of a fallible comfort zone
I must move from where I am
To get to where I need to be
Triumphantly making progress
A restless spirit being set free
To move from this place
Means really trusting God
To get me there

My Recycle

Recycle all my energies
Reroute my lonesome path
Rejuvenate all my desires
Unknowingly make me glad

Relieve me of worthlessness
Refuel me with positive things
I want to know real praise and worship
And soar on angel's wings

Redirect my spiritual focus
Oh Lord, teach me how to pray
Always standing in awe of you
Sowing goodness along life's way

Revive me with your spirit Lord
Immortalize my view
Keep me humble in my prosperity
For it all belongs to you

Water my seeds of purpose Lord
Dehydrate those seeds of doubt
Make plenteous my faith in your word
And on good soil, let those seeds sprout

Just Breathe

With a sigh of relief,
I let it all out…
Exhaling…
Out came worry
Out came stress
Out came all of the poisonous winds
That left my life in a mess
And when I inhaled…
Inhaling…
A fragrance that smelled of
Cool brook waters
A peaceful running stream
Honeysuckles and daffodils
Blue skies and butterflies it seems
A really calm wind that said it's okay now
Blades of tall grass
Just look at 'em sway
Blades like hands cheering "hip-hip hooray!"
I inhaled again
And I held my breath
As long as I could
I wanted it to last
Forever…
Like God promised it would
Oh to breathe again

Time Alone With God

Find it
Meditate
Restorer of virtue
Appreciate
In Him rest
Then sleep
And your soul
He doth keep
Talk with Him
Don't waste
Redefine
Make no haste
Listen
Read
Move
Take heed

New beginnings
His words, savor
Live again
In His favor
Time in Worship
Less lament
His will for your life
Just repent
Alone with God
Lifter of sin
Time well spent
Let Him in

I Hear You Speaking

I hear you speaking in the wind and rain
Even in the warmth of a summer breeze
Your love rings out in the ocean's tides
You are a towering lighthouse on stormy seas

Yet in the summer meadows of my tender years
Out where the wildflowers and crabgrass grows
I hear you speaking in the smell of honeysuckles
Amongst the thickets there, in a tiny red rose

In the quiet meadow, a shallow brook flows
The water is soothingly warm and crystal clear
What a beautiful place to find solace and refuge
My secret place in the springtime of the year

It's as awesome as a snowcapped mountain
When your profoundness reflects you there
Yet a flower blossoms deep in the valley
And its colorful fragrance just fills the air

I lift my face toward the sky and a subtle mist falls
A fresh anointing covers me like morning dew
Come Holy Spirit come, just breath on me
And I am restored all because...I've been with you

Earthen Treasures

Hope
Without it
I have nothing to live for

Peace
Because I have it
There's no need to cry anymore

Joy
Because he gives it
Nobody can take it away

Serenity
Because he grants it
Each and every time I pray

Love
Because he teaches it
Unconditionally, I can give it

Peace of Mind

My spirit is barefoot in
Summer's dew
The sweet aroma of peace soars
In the garden of my youth
I'm cultivating it like springtime
While the beat of my heart depicts a lyric
It stems from a repetitious repertoire of Grace
The honeycombs are filled to capacity
Like liquid gold from His personal reservoir
The story's old, and so often told
Yet un-like any known before
No fields or stones are left unturned
No need to toil or sift thru fertile soil
For my spirit sings out anew
As the sweet aroma of peace soars
In the garden of my youth

Lullaby My Soul

Lullaby my spirit Lord
Lullaby my soul
Take me in your arms Lord
Sing and make me whole

Lullaby my mind Lord
Keep it stayed on you
Melodiously have your way Lord
There's nothing I can't go through

Lullaby my body Lord
Help me to stay strong
Walk with me everyday Lord
Sing me a sweet love song

You've song through your angels Lord
They're all on one accord
If you sing to me in the midst of my storms
They won't seem so hard

You've song through the fowl of the air
They sang from atop their nest
I need to know that you are there Lord
Now sing to me so I can rest

Lullaby my problems Lord
Lullaby them all away
In your bosom I'll find sweet sleep
Tomorrow's a brand new Day

Just Be Still

I dared not move
From this place
It was his presence
That changed my pace
In awe of His Glory
I stayed right there
He ministered to me
Then made me heir
I knew I was where
He intended me to be
Like thunder he spoke
And speaking to me
I became real still…
While flashbacks of my life rolled,
for all to see
Thoughts undeserving
I couldn't help but cry
I was convicted…
He lifted me up
And gently wiped my eyes
I motioned for help from others
But there was no need
It was out of my hands
So I dropped to my knees
I've learned the Holy Spirit will speak
If we would just be still
When running on empty
Your vessel can be filled
I've learned to pray more
And worry lots less
Because it all belongs to him anyway
You can't help but be blessed
If you would just be still

Morals

Where are our so-called morals
How do we justify wearing his name
If we say that he has transformed us
How is it that we remain the same
Why is my brother still hungry
Why is my sister falling apart
Why does sin still fill our lives
And bitterness, our hearts
What gives us the right to play God
Does it make us appear to be strong
What justifies altering God's word
Making right appear to be wrong
Where do we go when the enemy strikes
Who gets the glory for our fame
Why do we laugh at another's downfall
How is it that we bear no shame
Where is God in our lives
Where are our morals?

My Spirit

Far beyond the highest mountain
As though I was destined from birth
My spirit now soars like an eagle
Rendering my soul from earth

Whisper a prayer I'm on my way
Removed are those doubts and fears
Buried hopes have begun to surface
Covered by the adversary for years

Removed are the things from my wings
Which often obstructed my sight
God's planned itinerary for this journey
Eases the turbulence of my flight

High above the birds of the air
High up above the wind and rain
Over the vast illustrious skies
Immune my body to physical pain

High above the darkest clouds
Far beyond the tallest trees
High above the largest crowds
And far beyond the restless seas

Higher than any man made object
The thunderous clouds doth roar
God has strengthened me for my journey
And now my spirit doth soar

About the Author

Among the lilies of the fields in the Deep South, a unique flower blossomed in every way imaginable. She went barefoot most summer days, climbed trees, fished, and swam in gravel pits, ponds, rivers and Florida beaches. She has a profound love for nature and family, and was quite gifted when it came to putting it into spoken words and pictures. She loved to write, draw and paint. Her artistical ability was well known in the community. She decorated high school doors at Homecoming, which often won first place. She drew cartoons for the high school paper. She wrote love poems and songs that were only recited within her inner circle, and now it is her season to shine.

Mary was born and raised in Atmore, Alabama. She is the seventh of eleven Children born to very loving and nurturing parents, Mr. and Mrs. Jethro Dailey Sr. She was a very active member of the Mt. Gilead Missionary Baptist church, under the leadership of the late Reverend Dr. N. L. Robinson. She is a 1978 Graduate of Escambia County High School, where she was very active: Cheerleader, majorette, powder puff football, Homecoming Queen, Who's Who among American High School Students, voted

Class Favorite, member of the Mighty Marching Blue Devils band and concert orchestra (oboe and glockenspiel), drama, sang with a local group "Nature's Gift" and excelled academically.

She was a Dean's List Student at Alabama State University, 1978-79. She continued her education at Alabama A& M University, where she not only earned a B.S. Degree but left a historical mark reigning as Miss Alabama A&M University, 1981-82, selected "Who's Who among American College Students" and member of Delta Sigma Theta Sorority, Incorporated.

She is a 1998 recipient of the very first prestigious Sui Generis "You Go Girl Award". She is also a 1999 recipient of the Fellowship International "Women of Excellence Award" for exemplary Christian service and commitment.

She has spoken on several Women's Day occasions and workshops in and around the city of Huntsville, Alabama where she has resided for more than 29 years. She has been employed for 25 years as a Supply Systems Analyst, Department of Army, Aviation and Missile Command, Redstone Arsenal, Alabama. She is an active member of the First Missionary Baptist Church, Huntsville, Alabama, Reverend Dr. Julius R. Scruggs, Pastor.

Her children include two biological treasures, Eric and Thaddeus Acklin and four extended treasures, Nicholas, Frederick, Steven and Travis Acklin.

Her hobbies include: Writing, reading, collecting porcelain dolls, miniature shoes, singing, sewing, painting, spending time with her precious "girlfriends", dinner and a movie night with the Dining Divas of Huntsville.

Her favorite passage of scriptures, I Corinthians 13, speaks of her unconditional love.